Ink from an Octopus

Leonard Gasparini

HOUNSLOW

Ink From An Octopus

ISBN 0-88882-117-4

Publisher: Anthony Hawke
Designer: Gerard Williams
Composition: Accurate Typesetting Ltd.
Printer: Gagné Printing Ltd.

Publication was assisted by the Canada Council
and the Ontario Arts Council.

Hounslow Press
A Division of Anthony R. Hawke Limited
124 Parkview Avenue
Willowdale, Ontario, Canada   M2N 3Y5

Printed and bound in Canada

Acknowledgements are made to *Antigonish Review,* *Canadian Forum,* *Canadian Literature,* *Quarry,* and *Toronto Life,* where some of these poems originally appeared — all in slightly different form.

To my sons, James and Lowell

Contents

Author's Note/1

I   Dream/5
Nocturne/6
Out of Time/7
"Seeking Whom She May Devour"/8
Adult Entertainment/9
Streets/10
Under the Ambassador Bridge/11
Nocturne for a Nun/12
La puttana Maria/13
The Visitant/14
The Death of Robert Desnos/15
Inscription/16

II   On First Looking into *The Horn Island Logs
of Walter Inglis Anderson*/19
Morning Worship/20
In the Tropics, I, II, III, IV, V, VI/21-26
The Sun Was a Lion's Head/27
Rattlesnake/28
Dead Opossums/29
Homage to Walter Anderson/30

III   Prelude to a Life/33
Toy Trucks/34
Still Life/35
The Old Barn/36
Weeds/37
The Earthworm/38
The Slug/39
The Centipede/40
Danaus Plexippus/41
Lines to a Ladybug/42
Crabdance/43
Pumpkins/44
Poinsettia/45
Moment/46

Notes/48

Author's Note

Most of these poems have been written in the last five
years, except for a few, written much earlier, but revised
for this collection.

I

Deep into that darkness peering, long I stood
there wondering, fearing...

Poe

Dream

In my dream, I clung to a broken spar —
Shipwrecked, naked, and weary —
Helpless as that sea turtle I saw overturned,
Its gashed neck bleeding on a white sand beach.
A tropic sun, blinded by its own reflection,
So blazed that sea and sky were one.
Did my aloneness and fear of drowning
Project the head of a swimming tiger?
A tiger swimming round in circles?
What fabulous beast, what sea-born sphinx
Was this before me? What strange omen?
The tiger swam until it found a focus,
Then glided, like a phantom, towards me.
We smelled each other's fear.
When the tiger clutched the spar
Our sense of fate was stronger.
I swear I saw the human in its eyes;
Perhaps it saw the wild animal in mine.

Nocturne

The rain plays softly on the attic roof.
The wet leaves of an ailanthus whisper.
Moths flutter at the window-screen.
The snake-hipped black woman rubbing her body with
    coconut oil
Gets up from the sofa to draw the bamboo blind.
There are moments when the flesh
Surprises my spirit into poetry —
And like a seed I inhabit a dark space
Made warm by the weight of my breathing.

Out of Time
To Donna

All summer I've lagged three hours behind you,
On Pacific time.
Your absence has thrown my timing off.
Whenever I glance at my wristwatch
I wonder what things you've already done
Or you will be doing, on Eastern time.
Sometimes we phone each other and forget whose time
    we're on.
Ours is a past-future relationship.
Do I think of you before or after you think of me?
I think love is a spatiotemporal phenomenon
That has frequent fits of relativity.
I am tired of clocks, calendars, tides, sunsets,
Daylight-saving time, timetables, and time zones.
I am tired of time all the time.
When I return to Toronto
We shall kiss till we turn to stone.

1986, Vancouver, B.C.

"Seeking Whom She May Devour"

How is it that her animal allure
Darkens my reason,
Makes me brood over trivia?
What kind of sorcery does she practise,
That my soul succumbs to pure desire,
And seeks in her an absolute?
(O goddamned succubus whose strange perfume is
    my fetish!)
How is it that she fevers my sleep
With her voodoo love dance?
Will I wake up dead or dreaming?

Adult Entertainment

In the close and sullen darkness
Of an all-night moviehouse,
Three men are making love to a woman
On the screen. There is a tremor

Of genitals, like sea anemones
Sucked by an undertow.
The audience watches this stark abstraction
Of flesh, breathing vicariously.

Each seems lost in himself —
A shadow that squints through a keyhole
At the shadows squirming within.
Lust festers at their feet,

And fantasy is triumphant.
The swollen darkness crouches like a cave.
If a match were suddenly struck,
The air would blaze with devils.

Streets
for Dôre Michelut

There are streets that follow us like shadows
Wherever we go; streets
That run our daily lives; streets
That corner us at night
When we are lonely or alone;
And there are streets that get lost too.

Under the Ambassador Bridge

I sat on a park bench
Under the Ambassador Bridge,
Watching people make pests of the gulls.
A bell buoy chimed.

The sun was sinking
Behind a factory in Detroit.
Sunk to its gunwales, a tugboat
Towing a rust-caked barge chugged by.

From the concrete jetty
A straw-hatted black man was fishing.
Not even the shadows
Of fishes were biting.

The river reeked of algae, oil, sludge,
And the bilgy wash
Of freighters steaming lakeward.
The western sky smoldered.

I thought of you then,
In the night of another city.
The bridge hovered over me.
A white feather blew along the bank.

Nocturne for a Nun

After the day's devotions
She goes for a solitary stroll —
Her veil afloat in the moonlight —
Fingering a black rosary.

She strolls through the convent garden,
Whispering *Ave Marias*.
A sudden breeze ruffles her habit.
She pauses to smell a rose.

And now the nun has a vision
Of love incarnate in Christ:
The darkness hidden inside the rose
For which the bloom is sacrificed.

La puttana Maria

She stared at the crucifix gleaming on the wall
Above her unmade bed
And remembered her first Communion
In an old Calabrian church.
Now the intinction was different.
Men came regularly to her monstrance of flesh
And received their favorite sacrament
On the altar of her bed.
                     The Eternal City
Had buried her innocence in a bordello.
Figlio di puttana! she cried,
Flinging a satin cushion at the Cross.

The Visitant

Why do you come, my enchanted one,
To visit me only when I am dreaming?
What sleep of mine creates your being?
What solitude of yours is buried in me?

And what happens to you when I waken,
And my soul, like an odor, stays behind?
Do you despair of your imaginary world,
Knowing you cannot enter mine?

The Death of Robert Desnos

When night came to Buchenwald
With lurid searchlights and wolflike guard dogs,
The poet looked for a hole
In the sky. It was not the moon
He saw among black clouds,
But his own skull wreathed with barbed wire.

Inscription

There is no evil so great
That love cannot accommodate.

II

My perfect rapport with nature came when I found my
first seahorse, the reconciling agent in time between the
horrible monotony of the machine and the bomb of
poetry — alive, and when I put it in water it hummed.

The Horn Island Logs
of Walter Inglis Anderson

On First Looking into *The Horn Island Logs*
of Walter Inglis Anderson
for Patricia

Much have I traveled in the natural world,
And many natural wonders seen;
Round an Ojibwa campfire have I sat
Listening to the music of trees,
As the wind plucked different chords from each;
Yet I never realized the beauty there
Till I read Anderson's *Horn Island Logs*,
And discovered that nature creates its own metaphors.

In the beginning was the image.
The imaged word I found
By going to the meadow, to the cactus desert,
To any uncultivated tract of land
And observing how wildflowers
Are pushed up by a chthonic hand.
The imaged word was a boat-tailed grackle preening his
    feathers
In a Mississippi salt marsh at sunrise;
It was a bull elk near Banff, bugling downwind,
With antlers the size of a rocking chair;
A sunny pond blooming with spatterdock;
Orange lichens eating into a weathered rock.
Seeing ripened my eyes; what I saw
Ripened within — until, with eyelids closed,
I believed I could smell the difference
Between a red rose and a white rose.

Morning Worship
for Salvatore Ala

This morning — after an interminable night
Of unutterable gloom — I looked out the window
And saw a robin hunting for earthworms
On the dewy lawn; I saw a cardinal,
With plumage as bright as his half-whistled song;
Two squirrels; a white cat pouring itself
Through a fence; and a monarch butterfly —
All existing in themselves
Among the trees and flowering shrubs.
I felt blest and gave praise to God.
The morning swelled like a choir inside me.

In the Tropics

I

In a tall dead tree
At the edge of the jungle
The *zopilotes* gather,
Waiting for death to feed them.

I hurl a stone at one of the black vultures
And narrowly miss.
It does not move,
But regards me as an intruder.

On an unpaved road that skirts the jungle
An iguana gasps, tail twitching.
It has been run over by a jeep,
And its guts glisten like jewelry.

The vultures unfurl their black umbrellas
And descend, circling lower
And lower
Till the road is a seething nest of shadows.

II

The road to Punta Morena plunges seaward
Through jungle. A scaly excrescence of rock
Flicks its tongue at an insect.
Ferns float on shadowy stems.
Scattered huts squat in the green heat of midday.
Beside the road, under a gum tree,
The sun-bleached bones of some animal
Burn like a white fire.

III

On this scorpion-tailed peninsula
Sleep the gods. Oh what can the gods say
Of this landscape haunted with ruins?
I climb the steep limestone stairway of a pre-Columbian
    temple
And gaze at the sea,
Listen awhile to the murmur
Of Yucatan's own coral-crusted shell.
Legend has it that anyone who stays overnight in Tulum
Is destined to go mad.
The ancient Maya painted sacrificial victims blue,
Adorned them with jade and gold
Before cutting out their hearts with a flint knife
And throwing the corpses into a sacred well.
Here beauty once flowered in death,
In homage to the god of rain.

IV
for J.C.

Although it is cruel, you cannot but marvel
At the ingenuity of Peruvian Indian children
Who have no toys to play with.
When evening comes they catch large-eared bats
With cicadas baited on fish-hooks,
And, attached to long strings,
Fly them like kites in the jungle.

V

To encounter a large land crab
Scuttling along the corridor
Of a seaside hotel in the tropics at night
Is a startling experience.
I can talk to a dog;
But a crab is so sensitive.
Both of us froze.
                              Suddenly
The crab sidled past me,
Keeping close to the wall,
Its pincers extended.
I followed the creature outside
To the edge of the patio,
Down a moonlit path,
Where it disappeared into a deeper shadow.

VI

From wintry skies the tourists come.
Jetplanes deposit them on the tarmac.
Dazzled by the Jamaican sun,
They grope for their luggage like pale larvae.

Out of step with the island's rhythm,
Shadowed by the stares of Rastas —
They devour the scenery and quickly burn;
Go native drinking white rum

And smoking ganja. They dodge
Patois-speaking higglers to embrace the beach;
Measure time by a bronze suntan;
Then fly home, flaunting it like a medal.

The Sun Was a Lion's Head

1 The sun was a lion's head
   Blazing down on the dry savanna.
   A sudden fire caught the grass;
   A herd of antelope exploded.

2 Over the rainforest canopy
   A crowned eagle soared —
   Then swooped. Its talons tore
   A small monkey from a treetop.

3 A strangler fig with aerial roots
   Thick as an elephant's trunk
   Formed a living coffin
   For the host tree it slowly crushed.

4 In the moist undergrowth
   A leaf-clinging leech tensed itself
   Like a twig, sensing the warmth
   Of a passing animal.

5 Night deepened the stillness
   To its roots. A sluggish river
   Shed the land like an old skin,
   And snaked seaward in moonlight.

Rattlesnake

I was riding shotgun with a stranger
through the flat Texas panhandle in the
quivering heat of a mid-August afternoon
my throat parched with dust and too many
cigarillos nothing but mesquite prickly
pear cactus for miles around suddenly a
rattlesnake slithered across the road
the stranger swerved his van to hit it
and missed.
            He found the rattler
Coiled in a clump of sagebrush,
And blew off its head
With one blast from his handgun.
Grinning like a good ol' boy,
He dangled his trophy in the air.
Ever eat snake? he said.
I saw his jack-knife flash,
As he severed the diamondback's rattle for good luck.
In my hand the rattle felt light as a pinecone.
It looked ancient, harmless —
Like some desert thing that died
Before man learned to kill.

Dead Opossums

Driving alone through the dusky backwoods
Of Alabama,
I saw a dead opossum on the road.
White beast, an Algonquian tribe named it.
The creature lay on its side — stiff legs extended —
Grinning like some misshapen, furry infant
With a long naked tail.
As my headlights hunted down others
In the moonless dusk,
I wondered if only their shadows
Were playing dead; and if so,
What shadow was playing with me?

Homage to Walter Anderson

To paint an octopus dying in the arms
Of its own iridescence
Was Walter Anderson's way of looking
Into the eye of God.

To make a "progress,"
He sailed his weatherworn skiff
To Horn Island — guided by pelicans
And the rhythm of a seahorse swimming on its tail.

To study the sequence of color,
He painted a Portuguese man-of-war stranded,
And its strange convulsion of form
When a wave washed over it.

Oh that we too might see the purpleness
Inside a dried mangrove root
When the wood is broken,
And dance for one endless moment
With a vision — holy and natural.

III

To see a World in a Grain of Sand
And a Heaven in a Wild Flower...
Blake

Prelude to a Life

This is my earliest childhood memory:
One rainy night
I refused to go to bed
Unless my mother let me throw our calico cat
Out of the upstairs bedroom window.

She handed me the cat.
I remember that it limped around our house for several
    days.
How this memory haunts me!
I think one must go into the unknown
To find something new.

Toy Trucks
for Lowell

He likes to play with toy trucks
And make his evening rounds.
He drives from room to room,
Uttering the strangest sounds.

The fire engine enchants him —
With ladders, hose, and bell.
The other trucks are traffic-jammed,
Forgotten for a spell.

A dump truck chips an earthen vase.
He lifts his drowsy head.
His mother puts the trucks away
And steers him straight to bed.

Still Life

Imagine a red-and-white checkered cloth
On a wooden table, and on the table
A bottle of homemade wine, bread, a dish
Of black olives, and Gorgonzola cheese.
Now try to imagine my octogenarian grandfather
Ringing a bell as he pushes his handcart
Through the streets of our neighborhood,
Sharpening people's knives. Imagine him
Returning home at noon to this still life,
And partaking of it with the gusto of an artist.

The Old Barn

The old barn sits in a field
Overrun with thistles and other tall weeds.
It clings to the landscape like an oak stump.
Emptied of everything but cobwebs, mice,
And the swallows that nest
Under its rain-sunken roof,
The old barn is a lost landmark.
The seasons stumble over it,
And trespass on the cropless acres
It once commanded.

Weeds

The weeds seem to multiply overnight.
Heaven knows we hoe them often enough,
Uprooting the most common
And troublesome ones.
Still they survive the hoe, the herbicide —
Holding their ground like they own it;
Disfiguring our lawns,
Suffocating our flowers.

It is not their appearance that offends us,
But lack of cultivation —
The way they invade our gardens
With such vigorousness.

Yet who are we to deny them wild growth?

Somehow I want to spare their weedy lives.
I want to call them by their proper names:
Lady's thumb, toadflax, shepherd's purse, goldenrod....

The Earthworm

To observe the common earthworm
Going about its earthy chores
Requires a fisherman's patience
Because it seldom goes outdoors.

This wriggly red invertebrate
Has no eyes, no ears, nose, nor chin;
But good heavens, it has five hearts!
And breathes through its sensitive skin.

The worm stays underground by day,
And surfaces mainly at night
To search for food, or find a mate —
Another moist hermaphrodite.

The Slug

Have you ever seen a slimy gray slug?
It isn't half worm,
Nor is it half bug;
But resembles a snail
Minus the shell.
Nocturnal by nature, a creature of damp —
This sluggish gastropod
Has a foot for a belly,
And drags the tide inland
With the slime from its body.

The Centipede

We seldom see the centipede;
When we do — it's unexpected.
It moves with such amazing speed,
All its legs seem disconnected.

The centipede lives under rocks,
And in the cellar of your house;
There it lurks, with long antennae
Less conspicuous than a mouse.

It has a pair of poison claws
That can inflict a painful bite;
So beware: this carnivorous chilopod
Always hunts at night.

Danaus Plexippus

The black-and-yellow striped caterpillar
Munching on a milkweed leaf
Is a living metaphor,
A master of regal disguise
That can metamorphose itself
Before your unbelieving eyes.

For the sake of a trope,
It will mummify its ghost
In a gold-speckled green cloak
(Like a trick suspended in time)
And emerge as a monarch butterfly;
Then migrate in fall to a tropic clime.

Lines to a Ladybug

The ladybug is a dainty beetle
With polka-dotted forewings;
And a welcome sight to gardeners
For the good luck it brings.
Look! the ladybug likes to walk
Upside down on a long leafstalk.
Although it's slow and often rests,
It rids most plants of insect pests.
Unlike the ant, it doesn't take
The honeydew that aphids make;
But in fruit tree and flowerbed
The ladybug eats the aphids instead.

Crabdance

At ebbtide, when the sun is low,
The fiddler crab emerges
From his mudhole
In a mangrove swamp,
Waves his large blue claw at the female,
And dances with his shadow.

Pumpkins

Under the harvest moon
A pumpkin patch glistens with dew
Where a shadowy scarecrow stands.
Pumped up by trailing vines,
The bee-pollinated pumpkins ripen
And grow plump. The October countryside
Bulges with orange rotundities
The wind cannot budge.

Poinsettia
Euphorbia pulcherrima

The December snow lights up the darkness.
The room is warm with the breath of Christmas.
A poinsettia glows in its clay pot on the table.
Look how each bract forms a fiery ray
Around a small yellow flower cluster,
And fans out into space — to the very edge
Of that space which the unpainted leaves darken
With their shadows. What a festival of light!
And from the strain of so much self-illumination
The plant's fragrance is exhausted.

Moment

The child looks at the ball.
The ball wants to play.

Notes

"Seeking Whom She May Devour": The title is a
translation of Baudelaire's Latin inscription on his
drawing of Jeanne Duval.

"La puttana Maria": The Italian expression "figlio di
puttana" means *son of a whore*.

"The Death of Robert Desnos": Robert Desnos was a
French surrealist poet (1900-1945).

"On First Looking into *The Horn Island Logs of Walter
Inglis Anderson*": This book was first published by the
Memphis State University Press, 1973. A revised edition
was published by the University Press of Mississippi,
1985.

"Homage to Walter Anderson": Walter Anderson was
an American painter (1903-1965). A "progress" was his
quasi-technical term for his method of wading, crawling,
and swimming among aquatic and amphibious creatures.
Horn Island lies off the coast of Mississippi.